KT-472-574

William Collins Sons & Co Ltd
London · Glasgow · Sydney · Auckland
Toronto · Johannesburg

Also compiled by Nanette Newman

THE BEST OF LOVE
GOD BLESS LOVE
LOTS OF LOVE
ALL OUR LOVE
FACTS OF LOVE

First published 1976
This impression 1986
© Bryan Forbes Limited 1976
ISBN 0 00 183980 2
Made and printed in Great Britain by
William Collins Sons & Co Ltd Glasgow

Vote for Love

when you vote you put a ✗ kiss next to the man you like best.

A collection of children's sayings
compiled by

NANETTE NEWMAN

COLLINS

Foreword

It was during a party for my youngest
daughter, Emma, that the talk strangely
turned to politics. Listening to a group
of young children trying to decide which
party to vote for and why, gave me the idea
that it might be fun to find out more about
children's attitudes towards those who govern
us. When one little girl said: "Why can't
they vote for love?" I knew I had the title
for the book.

On the face of it, love and politics are a
strange mixture, but then children's views
are a strange mixture. They combine innocence
with madness, occasionally a touch of truth
where we hadn't thought to look, and
uncontrived humour.

I would like to thank all the schools and the
numerous individuals who have given me such
help in putting together this further collection
of children's sayings on love, politics ...
and other things.

Nanette Newman

For Bryan with my love

Two Politicians loving each other.

My father says you have to watch out for a prime minister to tell the truth.

Benjamin aged 9

I think when you vote you have to do it in private. Its Like swearing

Jill aged 7

Doliticians are people Sometimes

Alison aged 9

My daddy Says he votes to go to the pub every night.

John aged 7

I bet if animals had votes they'd vote we didn't eat them

Carole aged 6

My dad works at being a striker and when I grow up I shall work there as well

George aged 6

A prime minister is so busy he doesn't have time to think

Bruce aged 8

My Friend says my dad is a red but he isn't he's a bus driver

Alex aged 7

If I had a vote, I'd vote for the christmas Party

Sandra aged 6

'oliticians are people who tell
other people to go to war

Anthony aged 13

Id vote to stop wars but
they Never ask you that

Mary aged 7

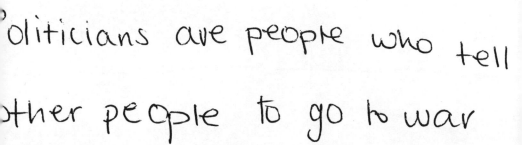

I went to the house of Lords
once, to watch the English play
the Australians

Kevin aged 8

My mum was in the Labour party when she had me born in hospital

Catherine aged 8

My Granny was a sufferer jet I think she flew a lot

Robert aged 7

I wish they wouldn't tax my daddy because it always makes him cross with me.

Robert aged 6

To get a vote you have to kiss old women and babies and that spreads deseese

Karina aged 7

Politicians Wave a lott when they tell you Bad news.

Elena aged 9

My auntie took me to the Soo and we saw too politishuns.

Katy aged 5

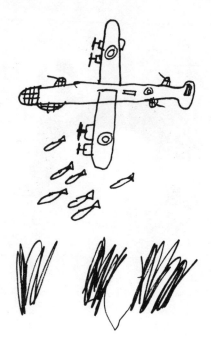

People blessed bombs during the war and
I think that's wicked,

Why cant you vote for
Love ?

Brenda aged 8

I never watch polliticks there
two dangerus

Rhodrey aged 5

When you grow up and get a job
the politicians make you pay
for their taxis.

John aged 8

I think rabbits make very good mothers

Sara aged 6

My dog wants to give all dogs he meets babies. Hes a terrible responsiblity

Albert aged 7

I had a baby budgie called Tabatha but she died before she knew what she was.

Ruth aged 8

My hamster went to heaven and came back a different colour.

Marilyn aged 6

Jesus could have been a pri minister if hed wanted To

Veronica aged 7

Good pepul aluays friten
bad pepul

Mark aged 7

It doesn't matter what you
believe, in as long as you
believe in something

Rosemary aged 12

Jesus wouldnt like the clothez now—they wouldnt sute him

Paul aged 5

Not many people vote for Jesus now because he didn't keep his promise

Gordon aged 7

I saw Jesus in the supermarket once. He was giving away soap powders

Lynne aged 6

when I was on holiday in France I
ate a lot of rhineoserous.

Clare aged 6

I dont like eating dead orange

Emma aged 4

My best friend is gradually becoming a brown person from India

Jane aged 6

My Sister and brother tell lyes it runs in the family

Laura aged 5

My big sister has gone To pot and prison

Enid aged 6

My mummy and
daddy are in luv
most of The Time but
when I go to bed they
Shout a lot.

Anne aged

I saw my sister fal
out of Love it was
very interesting

David aged

My friend wants to run away but he doesnt know where to go.

Tarmin aged 7

I went to my uncles wedding but I got sick so I suppose one he'll ask me to his don't next

Mario aged 6

my mum only likes
little babies. when they
get old Like me. she
smacks them.

Ronald aged 5

when I grow ~~up~~ up I Shall
have lots of babis, Then
I'll get married and liv
happily ever after.

Lisa aged 6

If my sister keeps on looking in the mirrer she'll Turn into a vanity

Susan aged 6

To get married you have to shave youre legs. I think

Alice aged 5

you have a hart attak if you fall in ove to kwickly

Paul aged 7

If you dont want to have a baby yo
have to wear a safety belt

Alison aged

Our doctor sais this
wont hurt while its
hurting

Christine aged 7

Even nasty people are nice
when you're ill

Marcus aged 8

I bit my doctor when
I was little but it didn't hurt

Katy aged 4

a dentist

The dentist makes you stay stiff. He is a kind gentleman

If heavens such a nice place why are people so sad about going there

Jennifer aged 6

I've been growing up all day

Emma aged 4

VE VOTE FO

TE FOR LOVE

LOVE VOTE F

VOTE FOR LO

FOR LOVE VOT

VOTE FOR LO

OR LOVE VOTE

VOTE FOR LOVE